END
TIME
DREAMS

Charleston, SC
www.PalmettoPublishing.com

End Time Dreams
Copyright © 2022 by Jeffrica Williams

All rights reserved

No portion of this book may be reproduced, stored in a retrieval system, or transmitted in any form by any means–electronic, mechanical, photocopy, recording, or other–except for brief quotations in printed reviews, without prior permission of the author.

Paperback ISBN: 979-8-8229-0948-9

End Time Dreams

Over 10 Years of Records

Jeffrica Williams

Table of Contents

Opening Prayer	1
Introduction	3
Seeing Myself	4
Eye in the Sky	5
Butternut Squash	7
Appointment with the Lord	8
Voice in the Cloud	10
The Clock	13
Power Outage	14
Water	15
Car Bombing	16
Fireworks	17
Chemical Attack	18
Deadly Virsus	20
Earthquake	22
Final Earthquake	23
Caught Up	24
Why Am I Here?	25
Babies in the Womb	27
Other Dreams	30
Ending Prayer	32
About the Author	33

Opening Prayer

Heavenly Father, I come to you with my hands lifted toward your holy oracle. My head is bowed to the only wise God, as I boldy approach your throne. I act in the spirit of obedience, have thine own way. I submit my agenda to yours; cancel any plans I have that don't line up with your will for my life. Kingdom of God come, will of God be done, in each and every one of our lives. Father, I have laid my truth out on the pages. Remove all lies and attacks from the enemy, that wants to steal our hope, kill your vision for us, and destroy our purpose. We shall rise from shame, doubt, insecurity and fear. We have overcome by the blood of the Lamb, and we shall be all that you have called us to be. This good work that you have started in us, it shall continue until the day of Jesus Christ. Take this small book, do as you see fit. It's out of my hands and into yours. In my Lord and savior Jesus Christ name AMEN!

Introduction

This book was already written. It's quite different from any ordinary book. Please grant me the grace for not having an author's language. My purpose is not to entertain, but to release. I have recorded everything just as I saw, no additional tales. Allow me to share this scripture from Jeremiah 23:32, *"Behold, I am against them that prophesy false dreams saith the Lord, and do tell them, and cause my people to err by their lies, and by their lightness, yet I sent them not, nor commanded them: therefore they shall not profit this people at all, saith the Lord."* My God, this makes me want to say nothing at all, but if what I say is true, then what is the fear about? For God does not give us a spirit of fear; I intensify boldness in my earthen vessel. This book will reveal over ten years of recorded dreams; some I have the exact date. These dreams don't happen all the time, just whenever God choses to share. At one point, I'd gotten so spoiled with this form of communication that I cried to God, when he was silent with this gift he blessed me with. I thought, surely he was frustrated with me, but that was my immaturity; thinking God didn't want to talk with his daughter. As I continue to grow in my walk with Christ, he is yet revealing, teaching and speaking. Allow me to share!

Seeing Myself

My eyes were in a space above ground beholding me on Earth. I didn't see the spirit of God next to me, but I felt his presence. It's like when a coach pulls a player to the side and starts showing him, what he's doing wrong in the game. He then tells the player what he actually should be doing to better the game. It was that sort of scenario, but without words. Some dreams don't need words, the spirit automatically knows. I detailed my appearance with this phrase.."I looked like Adam and Eve before they bit the fruit." When God first designed man, clothes were not part of the plan. Genesis 3:7 says, *"And the eyes of them both were opened, and they knew that they were naked; and they sewed fig leaves together, and made themselves aprons."*

I often prayed for God to show me what he thinks of me; that's the gentleness of a child wanting approval from her father. This was one of those moments where the coach pulled me aside. I saw the words that came out of my mouth and how I made two people in particular feel. I have two sisters on my mother side, they are so loveable and sweet, but like any other sisters, my goodness there have been challenging days. Out of anger, I have said things to them that were not pleasant or godly. My sisters admire and respect me, but it's really Jesus in me that makes them see me as light. So they hold me to a standard of santification, that's inspirational to them.

God showed me where his disappointment with my actions stood. For those of us who are saved, it really disappoints God when we disappoint his children. We are all God's children. In this dream, God allowed me to feel my sisters' emotions and the look on my little sister's face remains embedded in my memory. This dream was after our brother passed away. We had an argument over the phone, and I was yelling at her to the top of my lungs. What I said reached the ears of God. It wasn't about what my sister did, but how I chose to respond. We are held accountable for what we do and how we respond to what others do. I asked them both to forgive me. I recorded this dream 7/17/2017.

Eye in the Sky

One early morning around 4:30am I woke up drenched in sweat. I was shaking, my body felt like I had a fever of 101 degrees. I was breathing very fast as if I just ran 5 miles, as I so love to do. In this dream, I was outside playing basketball with my oldest son, Aj as we call him. He was getting upset at the game like he usually does, if he's losing. Suddenly, it became really dark outside. This was a thick darkness, a kind you don't see or literally can't see. I looked up and saw smokey clouds, a huge circle be- gun to form in the shape of a whirlwind. Out of this circle, a glowing blue colored light illuminated the sky, at that very sight I knew this was God. I instantly dropped to my knees afraid to look at this sight. You know what scripture that says, "every knee shall bow and tongue confess."

I truly understand why, your body knows it's creator. It doesn't matter what faith you have on this earth, your body knows that God is who he says he is. And when your body see it's creator, IT WILL BOW. My body automatically submitted to this glorious presence, that was so holy, so just and so pure. I remember feeling, "Why did I ever sin against this holy God?" I gripped my stomach in pain because my sins hurt me to the core. Everything I had ever done against God it hurt me. I was screaming and crying afraid to look up. I somehow got enough courage to glance at the sky; all I saw in that dark space was a huge eye. Please don't misunderstand me and say, "So God only has one eye?" I'm simply sharing what I saw. He was looking directly at me like no one else in the world existed. I tried to run telling my son to go, but he was already gone from my sight. This eye was so huge it could literally see the entire world without moving to the left or to the right, so where was I going? I ran to this stone wall, there is where I saw the light! Quicker than you can count to one, is how fast all my fear and pain left me at the sight of this light. Oh sweet Jesus I knew without a shadow of a doubt this was the light of the world. A peace came over me like a newborn baby being held by their mother for the very first time. Stay with me; while I was yet seeing this, I woke up in the dream. Meaning, it felt like I was woke, but I was still dreaming. I was trying to speak in tongues, but something was in my mouth. I kept trying to push the prayer through as I stumbled across my bedroom floor in search of the light switch. The light switch didn't work; I rushed to the hallway bathroom knocking things over on my dresser. I finally got to the toilet and vomited. This vomit was not natural; it was clear liquid that was not wet. The substance of it was not from food. After that bathroom situation, I really woke up this time. My mouth was wide open, like when someone is about to share their beverage with you and they say "hold your head back." Yeah that's real!

What I have written, is what I've seen

Butternut Squash

In 2021 during the season mushrooms sprout out the dirt, I dreamt of a fruit. This fruit looked like a butternut squash. I have never eaten one in real life be- fore. I had to google an image of what the inside looked like post having this dream. When I beheld it, I was like oh my, this is the fruit from my dream. The color was orange/yellowish, but it was big like a watermelon. I didn't recall eating this fruit, but apparently it was all finished. I was in my house scraping the seeds out of this fruit, to save them for later planting. The part that got me was that, I was saving the seeds. I felt like this was my new means of grocery shopping. I believe this dream was an answered prayer for a fragment of truth I was seeking God for.

When I woke out of my sleep, I started to reminisce over what God just showed me. I was reminded of the story of Joseph. Allow me to paraphrase it for you. Joseph was one of the twelve sons of Jacob, his favorite one; So much that he made him coat of many colors, meaning royalty. With Jacob favoring Joseph and God blessing him with the gift of dreams, his brothers were jealous of him. They wanted to kill him, instead they decided to sell him to the Ishmaelites; who took him to Egypt. After being sold into slavery, he was thrown into prison for refusing to sleep with the Potiphar's wife. She felt rejected, so she lied to her husband.

With God's help, Joseph interprets the dream of two prisoners. When it came to pass just as he predicted, one of the prisoners told Pharaoh two years after his release. At this time, Pharaoh was troubled in his sleep and needed interpretation. God revealed to Joseph the meaning of Pharaoh's dream. He told him there will be seven years of plenty, then there will be seven years of famine. Joseph tells Pharaoh they must save and put away for the seven years of famine. Read that last sentence again. Seeds are what I was saving.

What I have written, is what I've seen.

Appointment with the Lord

This next dream is a dream, that I like talking about. It can be really hard sharing your dreams with people. For some reason it puts the person listening and the person sharing in an akward space. Not only is the one person that's listening trying to hear it, but they try to make sense of it; with their own ideology. The person that's sharing the information is left wondering if they are coming off weird, or unbelievable. Well I don't feel any type of way about this one, as strange as it is, I like it!

I had this dream somewhere around my mid-twenties. I seemed to be back in my childhood apartment, where I lived with my mom, her boyfriend, two sisters and one brother. Even though it looked a bit different in the dream, I felt my childhood life. I just knew this was that apartment, even though it wasn't. I was on a payphone, as we had back in the day, I don't remember talking to anyone specific. A man appeared before me, I automatically knew he was an angel. Remember how I said, "some things the spirit just knows?" This was one of them, Allow me to describe this angelic man. He was tall but regular tall not like reaching to the heavens. He was dark complexed, bald- headed with a very strong face. His facial expression was fierce but gentle at the same time. I was not afraid. He looked like a human, there were no wings. He had on armor like clothing. He said to me, "You have an appointment with the Lord." I'll tell you, that's the only reason why I love telling this dream!

You know when they call you to the principal's office, if you've been behaving badly it scares you. However if you've been a good student, you're excited about meeting with the principal. I must have been a real good girl, because I was excited to go see the Lord!! Talk about boldness. When the angel said that to me, I just appeared in my bedroom. Scenes in dreams switch like movies. I started to pack undergarments the angel said "You won't need that where you are going." I then reached for my cellphone the angel said, "You won't need that where you are going." He said, "We must go to the waiting room." By this he meant living room. The living room was a small square space with a huge window and one couch. As we walked toward the living room me following behind him, I saw my little sister. Her name is Jerlmeka. She was standing in the bathroom combing her beautiful thick black hair into a ponytail. I've always loved her hair, it's so full and healthy. She was combing in a rush. I asked her,

"Where are you going?" She replied, "I have an appointment with the Lord too." As I walked into the living room or "waiting room" as he called it. I saw the angel staring out that huge window.

Without looking at me he said, "We must wait on a signal from the Lord." Let me tell you, when I looked out that window; it seemed like we were in the galaxy. I saw nothing but dark space and what seem to be stars. I sat on that one couch and my little sister came and sat right next to me. We quietly watched the angel as he stiffly stared out that window.

And then I woke up....MANNNNN!!!!! I was like wait, what happened to my appointment? I wanted to go back to sleep for a part two.

Listen, what I have written, is what I've seen.

Voice in the Cloud

During this time I was working at a hospital called, Delta Medical. I don't remember the year of this dream but, I was employed there from 2011 to 2014, so somewhere in that margin, a dreamed surfaced. Working at Delta is where I returned to Christ, I went through about six to seven months of backsliding, then Jesus knocked at my door. Let me take a moment to testify.

I knew better, so conviction hit me like a ton of bricks. My house was always full of people from: nieces, nephews, cousins, sisters, my kids, other people kids, etc. My point is it's very seldom, to be home alone in my house. But this particular day God came looking for me and I was home alone. Did you hear me? God came back for me. I know the scripture all too well now, Jeremiah 3:14 "Turn, O backsliding children, saith the LORD; for I am married unto you: and I will take you one of a city, and two of a family, and I will bring you to Zion." I was a backsliding child, who still went to church and very much believed. But my flesh wanted to taste a bite of the dusty earth. The flesh loves the things of the earth, the spirit loves the things of heaven. That's why flesh and spirit are always at war. That's another book that's needs a lot of unpacking. We get the point here, my flesh had won at this point in my life. But I'm valuable to God, I'm precious and marvelous in his sight. I belong to him and he knocked on my door to let me know. He caught me at a moment when I was home all by myself, and you want to know something? I was not thinking about God. This little girl that grew up always curious about God asking dumb questions, gazing into skies wondering, what's he doing this very moment. I thought if he's having a good day, now he catches me at a time where I'm in my sins'..ouchhh. That's exactly what I was getting from this unexpected visit. If you are caught doing what you're doing now, you want be ready. One day Jesus is coming for his church, but I will talk more about that in another dream. We must rise up from a lifestyle of sin and fulfill our purpose here on Earth. We have gifts and callings that we are sitting on, and God is not pleased. Assignments have been pushed to the back of the to do list and God is not pleased. Who will go? There's a scripture out of the book of Revelation chapter 3 verse 20 "Behold, I stand at the door and knock: if anyman hear My voice, and open the door, I will come in to him, and sup with him and he with me." I am a living witness of that knock. Let me tell you, it wasn't pretty. My father came back to get me with a belt, like a runaway child. This is my testimony, I will tell you now; I got a spiritual whooping from my father. Grace and mercy was all in that whooping, and I'm thankful for it everyday. I was crying, kicking and and screaming in my living room floor saying, "I'm sorry God, I'm sorry, pleaseeee I'll change my ways." That's the short version of this huge pivotal turn in my life called, REPENTANCE.

My co-workers at this hospital witnessed this transition in my life. After that whooping I got off that floor never to be the same. However righteousness was not laid out like a red carpet for me to easily walk on. It's something that I continue to pursue daily. With that being said, let's get to the dream.

I was placed on a high cliff, before my eyes was nothing but power. That's the only description I can use to identify with what I was beholding. I saw thick, gray like-clouds that filled the air, I heard sounds of wind moving. All of this power at this moment was created just for me to see. I saw a face form in a huge cloud to the right of me looking forward, as a matter of fact in the same direction where I saw the eye. This time it was a face but I couldn't make out the details of it, I just knew it was there. Then I heard a voice that had the echo of a loud microphone yet gentle. Now I have no idea why, but the voice slightly resembled my pastor's voice. The first part of this conversation was erased from my memory the moment I woke up, so I'll use the words: this or that to complete the sentence.

The voice exclaimed.."I love it when you do this." "I love it when you do that."

"I don't like the way you act when you are at work." Let's breath for a second.....I can't remember one thing that God said he liked about me but I will never forget these words.

"I don't like the way you act when you are at work." I believe God purposely blocked out the first part of that conversation from my memory.

He knows I would potentially overdue these good qualities; now turning them into idols. I only remember, "I don't like the way you act when you are at work." Now we're talking about the saved, born again Christian that sat in floor for a couple of hours kicking, screaming and repenting. The girl that's inspiring and motivating, everyone around her. The one people are asking to pray for them on the job, the one that God is using to lay hands on the sick and to heal people. The one that'll give her last dollar, always paying for people's food and bringing food. I'm one of the best workers, and God doesn't like the way I act at work?

Honestly, I didn't replay all that in my head. I quickly examined my work behavior, and asked myself "what am I doing at work?" Ready for some truth..? Maybe it's the entertainment and participation of gossip. Maybe it's the pleasure of allowing men to flirt with me, and I'm a married woman with children.

Maybe it's the Youtube videos, I shouldn't be watching on my cellphone. Maybe it's my smart mouth that always has to let somebody know I'm not the one to play with. I said to myself, "Jeffrica take your pick." When you are chosen by God to be set apart, you must take up your cross and follow Christ. To be like him, acknowledge him all your ways. We don't want to misrepresent Jesus, and send confusion to the minds of those that are watching.

Prime Example: Before the knocking on the door part, that I previously testified about happened. I was a fighter, I mean a "what you wanna do?" type fight- er. I had a mouth, and a swing to back it up. Even in that God was raising up a warrior. When I learned, I could no longer fight with my hands it became frustrating, I wanted to land a one, two real quick. One time I went to my car in that Delta parking lot to let out a scream, "SO GOD I GOT TO BE A PUNK?" I believe he understood my frustration even though that was an inappropriate comment.

I know my father was in the clouds like, "watch what I do with that fight you got." Since then I've been going to war. The enemy never gets tired. When I get knocked down, I hop back up with a mean prayer; after I'm done I go, "POW TAKE THAT!" Yep, with a mean face.

The saints say, "You just gave the devil a black eye."

The Clock

There was a huge digital clock floating back- wards in slow motion, in the midst of the air. I saw ten seconds on the clock and it went down to nine like 00:09. I heard the ticking sound that you hear clocks make. I saw what looked like a group of an- gels flying across the sky, toward the eleven o'clock direction. They were bright, but their wings weren't moving. In the human mind it looked like a lot of lit up airplanes. I heard a loud siren, such as when you hear a tornado warning. I thought, "Oh my, Jesus is coming." I appeared in a room; I suppose it to be my childhood home. My family was there laying fast asleep, I mean that hard type of sleep. I don't remember seeing my kids, just my family I grew up with. They were scattered across the room floor. I was yelling to them, "GET UP AND REPENT!" I kept saying, "JESUS IS COMING, REPENT!" My family wouldn't move a muscle. I even picked one of their limbs up; it just flopped back down the floor. Although I didn't like the sound of that, this is what I dreamt.

What I've written, is what I've seen.

Matthew 24:36 But of that day and hour knoweth no man, no not the angels of heaven, but my Father only.

Power Outage

On July 6, 2022, I woke up from a dream. For a while now, people have been predicting a world wide power outage to happen in our near future. This is what I dreamt, an earthquake hit the land. When it shook the Earth power lines bursted, and everything went dark. I'm unclear if this power outage was world wide or nation wide. For a moment the only light was from the stars in the sky. People quickly found ways to adjust. I remember walking around in the dark stunned at the people's behavior. I couldn't have imagined how Moses really felt when he came off that mountain. The same children that God just delivered out of that hands of Pharaoh were now partying like they didn't just witness power at it's highest. I mean they seen the plagues, they witnessed the miracles; they are now free, but still went to build themselves another god. I was walking around in that dream wondering, "we have no power and people still out here selling food;" markets were set up like you see in village towns. Clothes were hanging everywhere, it looked like a mess.

    I couldn't smell in the dream but if I could, I'm sure it would smell like a pig sty. People were going on with their regular lives instead of asking God for forgiveness. At one point, I believed I heard a radio and people blasting music. Tents were set up outside, people were busy as usual. When I woke up from that dream, I was reminded of the scripture Jesus spoke about in Matthew 24:36- 39, *"But as the days of Noah were so shall also the coming of the Son of manbe. For as in the days that were before the flood they were eating and drinking , marrying and giving in marriage. Until the day that Noah entered into the ark. And knew not until the flood came and took them all away: so shall also the coming of the Son of man be."*

    What I've written, is what I have seen.

Water

If you have been paying attention to what's going on around the world, then news of a water short- age would not be a surprise to you. Sometime in 2021, I dreamt that our water system was purposely being contaminated. Yep you heard right; not by dying fish or whales, but it was ordered. At least that's what I sensed. I saw two men in black uniforms, fair skin complected pouring what look like huge bags of salt into the water pipes. These are the same type of men I have seen in several dreams chasing me. In January 2021, I saw the same image of men chasing me, I ran to find a place to hide. One soldier looking guy held a gun up to me but I always seemed to ecsape. That was the end of that dream.

Matthew 6: 25-26 "Therefore I say unto you, Take no thought for your life, what ye shall eat, or what ye shall drink; nor yet for your body, what ye shall put on. Is not the life more than meat, and the body than raiment? Behold the fowls of the air: for they sow not, neither do they reap, nor gather into barns; yet your heavenly Father feedeth them. Are ye not much better than they?"

What I've written, is what I've seen.

Car Bombing

This dream was more than five years ago. I saw the destruction of cars right before my eyes; I was in the midst of it. The scenery looked like a war was happening. I heard loud sounds of shooting bombs, it sounded like guns were firing, and car alarms going off. Chaos and engine smoke filled the atmosphere. This was done by man's hand and the use of machinery weapons. It felt as if transportation was being wiped away from history and no longer allowed. Again, one of those guys from the other dream started to chase me and I ran under one of the blown up cars. I saw their boots as they were passing me. I remember heavy breathing of panting coming from me. Although, I appeared to have a sense of bravery and courage. That's all I saw of that dream.

What I've written, is what I've seen.

Fireworks

I recall having this type of dream twice; since they're so similar I'll share the one that I have more details about. Every 4th of July here in the Memphis, people gather in the downtown area to see the huge firework show they put on for the city. They have the really big ones, with extremly loud pops and bright sparkles. These are the types of sparks I remember seeing in the dream. The sparks went up into the air making a loud shooting sound; landing into the waters of the Earth. When the sparks hit the waters of the Earth. the entire body of water lit up like thunder. It looked like electrictity, when a plugged in radio hit the tub. I dreamt of this scene twice, that's why I decided to share it. I believe God was sharing something with me, concerning this dream. I have no idea of what, but he is yet revealing, speaking and teaching. I recorded this 8/16/2021.

What I've written, is what I've seen.

Chemical Attack

I recorded this dream in the early morning of November 14, 2021. I will try my best to be very detailed about this one, I believe this dream was an answered prayer. I saw a black man extremly angry about a situation with his job. I knew he had a very important position but I'm unsure of what level of authority. He was wearing a suit, but because of his rage the jacket was off, and the long white button down shirt was half tucked. I remember two people being with him, like there always are with an important per- son of power. I remember seeing a brief case, I think it was thrown to the ground during his temper tantrum. He said some words, then fired a chemical into the air, such as when a person fire a gun upward. A great number of people in that surrounding town became very sick. I remember it being breaking news on a televison screen that appeard before my eyes, in the midst of the sky. I heard a news broadcaster speaking on the matter, and they showed sickly people laying around. Some people skin started to peel off their bodies, and they were crying out in agony. It looked like an acid attack.

I'm not saying that's what happened, I'm just describing what felt familiar. The effect of the chemical seemed to destory cells in their brain. They where generated a virus. However, the man became infected by his own action. He came to what looked like a clinic, there were nurses working in the lab behind a glass window. People were lined up along a wall to the left of my view, crying for help. There was a nurse working there; she knew who this man was, he came for her. She rushed over to him, he was trying to tell her how to save his life. He was grasping for air, almost dead. The nurse bent down to kiss him, he gained a little strength. She starts to solve an equation with her words in a thinking out loud manner. It reminded me of that movie, The Nutty Professor, where only Clump, and his inner character knew this secret formula, and how to interpret the equation.

I specifically remember the lady speak the word, ph2. She yelled a few words of medical terminology to the other workers in the lab.

Behind that glass, they started to formulate a vaccine. A worker came from behind the glass, and handed a needle to the nurse. She gave the man a shot. Immediatley after I saw that, the dreamed switched.

A birthday cake was presented in front of me. I knew the cake was for me, even though I couldn't see myself. It's as if I was watching from somewhere in the spirit. That's all I remember from that dream.

When I woke up out my sleep, I started to research ph2. I randomly came across a professor teaching about a virus that infected over a million people. This was report- ed on March 24th; That's the day of my birth. However this particular virus was found in the food, not in the air.

What I have written, is what I've seen.

Deadly Virsus

Hearing these types of things can be difficult, and even hard to believe. One thing I love about my mother, she doesn't like to hear such things, but she believes. God is gracious enough to share with us, when he doesn't have to. What if no warnings came before destruction..My God! Lord we thank you. On the morning of December 25, 2021, I was awaken from another dream that left me startled. Sometimes I see myself in my body in dreams, other times I don't see me at all. In this particular dream, I saw myself. This world didn't look the same; it looked demolished. The scenery reminded me of that movie, "The Book of Eli." I was standing in an apartment complex. (By the way) I've had several dreams where I was in an apartment complex. I grew up living in apartments, I'm sure that probably has a lot to do with it.

Again, I was standing in front of this girl outside of these apartments. She was crying as she held her arm out to me. She said, "they bit me." I knew she meant the people that looked like zoombies. I know, but stay with me here. I knew this was a spread of another dealdy virus. This was a vicious scene. It seemed as if these people were trying to bite human flesh. They specifically wanted those who had not been affected.

They had a mangled walk, and distorted faces that you might see in movies. I saw the girl's arm, it instantly turned purple and red. She became one of them. They started to come for me, I took off running. Because of their drag, it was difficult for them to catch up with me. As I was fleeing help was provided for me along they the path I was running. Weapons were on the ground for me, I came to car that had keys in it. I remember crying so hard in great fear for my life. I heard a voice ask, "When will the end be?" This question reminded me of that scripture out of the book of Revelation chapter 6 verse 10.

"And they cried with a loud voice, saying , How long O Lord, holy and true, dost thou not judge and avenge our blood on them that dwell on the earth?"

When I heard that cry in my dream, "When will the end be?" a voice responded out the sky. It said, "When people began to flee to the east."

I got into the car and began to drive away, a feeling of peace overcame me. I knew I was going to be okay. When I woke up from that dream, I wanted to research the people fleeing to the east. I always read my bible after having these type of dreams. Just a chapter over in the book of Revelation, from where I read about the cries of the souls that were slain, I read someting interesting in chapter 7. Allow me to share.

Revelation 7:2 *"And I saw another angel ascending from the east, having the seal of the living God: and he cried with a loud voice to the four angels, to whom it was given to hurt the earth and the s e a ."*

Now if you haven't already studied the book of Revelation, you might want to give it a shot and pray for understanding. I would recommend you take some time to read Chapter six and seven of Revelation, before reading about the next few dreams.

What I have written, is what I've seen.

Earthquake

I recorded this dream January 24, 2018. In the middle of the night, I arose out of my sleep. An earthquake had hit a popular downtown area, I'm unsure of where. I saw a tall building swaying slowly from side to side, as it appeared that it was going to fall over. There were people running, trying to escape the danger. I saw people either running or jumping out of windows. This tragedy was broadcasted live over the news as chaos filled the atmosphere. I saw myself holding a baby in my arms, begging God for forgiveness. I wanted to make sure that if this was my time, I would be with him in paradise. I don't under- stand why I was even in that dream, because that city didn't seem to be where I currently live. I began to see things in flashes that didn't make sense to me. I saw people taking their love ones out of the hospitals in a rush. I saw a celebrity figure that I actually liked when I was really into secular music. I saw boats and ships being trapped in the sea. This was a devastating sight.

What I have written, is what I've seen.

Final Earthquake

I recorded this dream August 8, 2017. I believe this was a revelation given to me in regards to what I was studying at that time. In a dark space, I saw a large iron top that halfway opened a whole to the ground revealing fire underneath. You know those manholes in the streets covering the ground where sewers are? That's the image that came to my mind, only this was bigger. This next image is very faint, so I apologize for the lack of detail, but it seemed to be the presence of God seated on a throne, with his right foot on the top of that iron manwhole looking thing. It's as if he used his foot to slightly open that whole. I heard these words, "There will be a final earthquake before the coming of my Son." When I arose out of my sleep, I opened my bible to the book of Revelation. I read Chapter 6 allow me to share verses 12-17.

"And I beheld when he had opened the sixth seal, and lo, there was a great earthquake; and the sun became black as sackcloth of hair, and the moon became as blood; And the stars of heaven fell unto the earth, even as a fig tree casteth her untimely figs, when she is shaken of a mighty wind. And the heaven departed as a scroll when it is rolled together; and every mountain and island were moved out of their places. And the kings of the earth, and the great men, and the rich men and the chief captains, and the mighty men, and every bondman, and every free man hid themselves in the dens and in the rocks of the mountains; And said to the mountains and rocks, Fall on us, and hide us from the face of him that sitteth on the throne, and from the wrath of the Lamb. For the great day of his wrath is come; and who shall be able to stand?"

When reading the bible we have to understand when God is speaking symbolically or literally.

What I have written, is what I've seen.

Caught Up

Over the past ten years maybe even before, I've been having several dreams of being caught up. That's the real reason behind that hissy fit, I shared in my testimony earlier in the book. I didn't want to be left behind for the great tribulation, so I was begging as if the portal was open. Please God Please!! I tell you we better pray now, because when the books are open, Lord have mercy. Each time that I dreamt of being caught up, it wasn't a fast snatch. I say that because that's how we envision it, according to how we read the scripture. Let's read it together, 1 Corinthians 15:52 *"In a moment, in the twinkling of an eye, at the last trump: for the trumpet shall sound, and the dead shall be raised incorruptible, and we shall be changed."*

So for this reason we all picture a quick snap, and it could very much happen that way. However, I saw a graceful and happy floating type of motion. Everyone that was going up, they knew exactly why! Everytime I went high enough, I woke up. I remember saying in one particular dream, "I hope it's foreal this time, please let it be real!" The float upward was so peaceful and nothing on the earth matters, you can't wait to get there. I remember feeling disappointed in one particular dream as I was slowly being let back down. It was like I saw Jesus and his hand stretched out to me. I saw others with him, but I have no detail of their faces. I felt as if they were saints from the Earth. Now I'll segue this into my next dream.

Why Am I Here?

In this particular dream of being caught up, I was standing outside of the home I live in now. As I was looking into the night skies I saw a very small sample what John described in Revelation chapter six. Oh I'm sure I got the light version, because Lord knows; I'm no John. I need to make that crystal clear! Let's read the scripture again together. It's very important that we catch this. Revelation 6: 12-17

"And I beheld when he had opened the sixth seal, and lo, there was a great earthquake; and the sun became black as sackcloth of hair, and the moon became as blood; And the stars of heaven fell unto the earth, even as a fig tree casteth her untimely figs, when she is shaken of a mighty wind. And the heaven departed as a scroll when it is rolled together; and every mountain and island were moved out of their places. And the kings of the earth, and the great men, and the rich men, and the chief captains, and the mighty men, and every bondman, and every free man hid themselves in the dens and in the rocks of the mountains; And said to the mountains and rocks, Fall on us, and hide us from the face of him that sitteth on the throne, and from the wrath of the Lamb. For the great day of his wrath is come; and who shall be able to stand?"

In my dream, I saw stars falling from the sky, the heavens rolled up like a scroll. I saw a light; I knew this was the Son of God, who died on the cross and rose again for the remission of sins. I saw people running, trying to hide themselves, but my eyes were fixed on Jesus bursting through the sky. In-stead of me being excitied like in previous dreams, I was standing there puzzled asking, "Why I am here?"

According to what I believed my entire adult life, I should have been raptured out a long time ago. I knew that I had been facing tribulations. I don't know how I knew, but like I previously stated, some information in dreams, the spirit just automatically knows. When I woke up I started to research the scriptures for myself. I started praying for God to reveal truth unto me, "please Lord help me understand." God started waking me up early in the morning like 3:00am. Sometimes I wouldn't stop studying until about 8:00a.m. I would do what I needed to do, then get right back at it. Time was flying; I actually found joy in studying the word of God. Most people stay away from the book of Revelation, but it's the book I've probably studied the most along with the book of Daniel. I wasn't looking to be right, I was in search for truth. I wanted it, I needed it, I prayed for it, "God don't let me be deceived." Believers are divided with a pre-trib or post-trib theology, concerning a timeline that I don't believe is on God's clock.

Allow me to share some scriptures I dissected to under- stand this dream God had given me. Because that's just the kind of God we serve, he wants us search the deep things about him. The bible says in 1 Corinthians 2:10 *"But God hath revealed them unto us by his Spirit searcheth all thing , yea the deep things of God."* It's time we come off the milk and get the meat. We are living times of the beginning birth pains. These dreams are for the End Times.

If we sincerely pray to God for answers, he will respond. Our God is alive! Amen somebody! We serve a living God, and I'm glad about it. God will give you revelation and other people will be wondering, "how did you get it?" So open your bible and read over these scriptures. Break it down, unpack it, eat it, swallow it, digest it, whatever you have to do; just get an under- standing.

Matthew 24: 4-44

1 Corinthians 15: 51-54

1 Thessalonians 5:2-11 2 Thessalonians

2 1-12 Revelation 6, 7, 12, 13

What I have written, is what I've seen.

Babies in the Womb

Now I was not prepared for this particular season in my life. Spiritual birthing; I'd never heard of such a thing until I became pregnant. Out all of the Sunday school classes, bible studies, and sermons, I could not recall one time hearing about being spiritually pregnant. I have been under awesome leadership through out my young life, but I guess God was holding this for me to experience myself. I thought, if this wasn't taught then it must be a myth or something. Is this one of those spiritual things that people just made up? I pondered if this was biblical or not. I'm one of those type of people that has to always look for the answer in scripture. I read some scriptures that metophorically speaks of spiritual birthing such as; Isaiah 66: 7-12

"Before she travailed, she brought forth; before her pain came, she delivered of a man child. Who hath heard such a thing? Who hath seen such things? Shall the earth be made to bring forth in one day? or shall a nation be born at once? for as soon as Zion travailed, she brought forth her children."

There is a story about the the travailing woman in Revelation 12. That takes a lot of studying to comprehend. We should study to show ourselves approved, so I'll let you read that in your own bible study session.

Now back to the babies I dreamt about! I've had several of these dreams, I've actually lost count. These dreams would be so intense, that I would be seeing a baby moving in my womb and I would be feeling it in reality. I have three beautiful children, I know what a moving fetus feels like. Besides having an excuse to be greedy, feeling my natural baby move was my most favorite part of being pregnant. I never got tired of the baby moving around, I would constantly pull my shirt up to watch the activity. It didn't even matter to me where I was, if my baby was moving, I was watching. There were times when I would feel movements in my stomach but there was no fetus. If I told this to someone they would say, "oh you just have gas," But they didn't understand, how could I blame them? Even the scripture said the same thing I did; "Who heard of such thing?" I do understand Isaiah was recording an entirely different situation, stay with me. Years later, now I hear about it all the time. I dreamt I gave birth to three babies, all three different shades and colors. This part sounds crazy, but one of the babies came out of my stomach and started walking off. One baby was so beautiful with blue eyes.

Another baby's hand came out of my stomach. These babies never came out of the part where women naturally give birth; they literally came out of my stomach. I started to feel like I was pregnant in real life, bloated belly and all. I would be laying in my bed and feel tense movements in my stomach. I became curious about this whole situation, and wanted to understand what is going on here.

So I started to do some research and I came across other women of faith testimonies about being spiritually pregnant. Thank God for the courage and honesty of those women, because other young women like me are reading their stories. Maybe my honesty about these dreams will encourage others to know, you are not crazy!

I completely understand the not wanting to share part, and maybe it's not time for you to share. I believe there was a time when I moved too fast, and it cost me embarassment. Here is the thing, I learned our womb is also a place where we give birth to purpose. God will place a special assignment in the belly of our soul, in due time we must give birth to it. The process of this pregnancy can be uneasy due to the stretching hand of God. We must protect his plan, with prayer and patience. The delivery will happen just when we have dilated long enough for it's appointed time. If we move too soon and go ahead of God's timing, we can abort his plan. I had a dream where I was carrying, a breathless baby into an emergency room. I had just given birth at my home, and it was now gone. That's why I stated, I believe there was a time when I moved ahead of God. In January of 2021, I dreamt of another pregnancy, I went into a clinic and this woman did an ultrasounds on my belly. This was done in the spirit because she never ouched me. On a huge screen a sweet looking woman appeared in brigh light, wearing a white doctor's jacket. She had beautiful hair that came down to her shoulders. She looked at me and said, "You are fifteen weeks pregnant." My reaction was so comical, that it put a smile on the woman's face. I was being my silly self saying, "Ohh Lord nahh nahhh I can't have another baby." The woman smile was so beautiful. She nodded her head and said, "Yes you are fifteen weeks pregnant." Six months later I held my first Women of God Power Circle meeting. One year before that I opened my own business. So you tell me if spiritual birth is real or not!

What I have written, is what I have seen.

Other Dreams

Since I was a teenager, I can remember different dreams that seemed supernatural. Throughout my life, God would chose to show me different people and what might be bothering them at the moment. I have learned to be bold enough to reach out and give a few words of encouragement. I'd even write a letter to God or pray for their situation. The responses of the people gave me clarity that my dreams are real, and God is serious. I have had a few dreams of floodings, storms, hurricanes, and tsunamis in the past.

My prayer is that these dreams don't scare you wrong but straighten us all right. God said in his word that he would pour out dreams and visions. So why are we hesitant to believe when he actually does? It's easier to believe a lie than to accept the truth. I pray that when God see's me, he doesn't see Jeffrica, but that he sees his son. Jesus went to the cross for me, he was raised up for me, and I believe I will be raised up to meet him in he air. I'll leave you with this last dream.

I saw a scene from the bible days, when Jesus was preaching to the people. I saw the disciples surrounding him. Jesus stood a couple of inches taller than the other men in the crowd. His back was facing me and he was preaching to the people. No! He was not talking in a quiet or peaceful manner, he was speaking with great authority. His back was strong and muscular. His shoulders were broad, he was wearing a light brown coat, the kind you see in those old bible movies. This scenery looked as if those Phar- isees and Sadducees were questioning him about something he said. I wasn't able to pick up what was being said, but I got a very small glimpse of Jesus' face. With his back toward me he turned and looked over his right shoulder. I saw that Jesus had a beard and sort of shoulder length hair. I know there a lot speculations out there about how did Jesus really look, was he black or was he white. I once heard a pastor say, "Jesus can appear to different people, in different lighting." John saw him in all his glory, in the book of Revelation chapter 1: 14-15

"His head and his hairs were white like wool, as white a snow; and his eyes were as a flame of fire; And his feet like unto fine brass, as if they burned in a furnace; and his voice as the sound of many waters."

The Jesus I dreamt about had to between 30 to 33. He looked neutral, and earth toned to me. That's the best I can describe what I saw. I'm no scientific genius, but I believe the pigmentation of human's skin color was little bit different over 2,000 years ago. The point is for us not to worry about what he looked like, but what he did. How he was shown to me could be different from what God choose to share with someone else. When Mary saw Jesus at the tomb, I don't believe she saw the same Jesus John beheld in Revelation.

If you don't take anything away from this book, take this; JESUS IS ALIVE AND HE WILL RETURN AGAIN. RIGHT AWAY!

REPENT OH YEAH NATIONS, RUN RUN RUN OUR REDEEMER DRAWS NIGH!!! May the love of Christ be with us all. Amen!

Ending Prayer

Heavenly Father, it is done. I have completed this assignment! Oh my Lord, I pray that you are pleased with it, and that you see I have handled it with pure intentions. Bless every reader in the name of Jesus. I pray miracles fall upon the people even now; spiritual miracles, financial miracles, healing miracles, and awakening miracles. I pray restoration and reconciliation in the name of Jesus. I pray an increase of faith has been shifted. I pray a desire to understand your word be burned into our hearts. I pray truth be revealed to your people, and those who have the gift of dreams and visions will no longer be restricted by fear or intimidation from the world. It's not about our feelings, it's about the work that must be accomplished. I pray the lost will come to know your son and accept Jesus as their Lord and savior Amen!

About the Author

Jeffrica Williams is a wife and mother of three kids. She had a very normal childhood. Going to church was something she really enjoyed doing. Without being taught of God's existence, she already knew in her young heart that HE IS! She had a desire that lit a fire on the inside of her to gain knowledge of this mysterious God. Little did she know one of his intrinsic ways of communication was predestined for her life. She was baptized as child, but officially accepted Christ into her life at the age of 16. Like every other Christian, she is just waiting to get home. In the meantime she is determined to fulfill her purpose here on Earth.

> *Habukkuk 2:2-3*
> *And the Lord answered me and said, Write the vision, and make it plain upon tables, that he may run that readeth it, For the vision is yet for an appointed time, but at the end it shall speak and not lie: though it tarry, wait for it; because it will surely come, it will not tarry.*